Young
Thurgood Marshall

Fighter for Equality

A Troll First-Start® Biography

by Eric Carpenter
illustrated by James Watling

Troll Associates

Library of Congress Cataloging-in-Publication Data

Carpenter, Eric.
    Young Thurgood Marshall: fighter for equality / by Eric Carpenter;
illustrated by James Watling.
        p.   cm.— (A Troll first-start biography)
    Summary: Examines the life of the first black man to be appointed
an associate justice of the highest court in the country.
    ISBN 0-8167-3770-3 (lib. bdg.)   ISBN 0-8167-3771-1 (pbk.)
     1. Marshall, Thurgood, 1908-1993—Juvenile literature.   2. Judges—
United States—Biography—Juvenile literature.   [1. Marshall,
Thurgood, 1908-1993.   2. Judges.   3. United States.   Supreme Court—
Biography.   4. Afro-Americans—Biography.]   I. Watling, James,
ill. II. Title.   III. Series.
KF8745.M34C37   1996
347.73'2634—dc20
[B]
[347.3073534]   95-10023
[B]

Thurgood Marshall was the first African-American elected to the Supreme Court—the highest court in the United States.

Thurgood was born in 1908. He lived with his mother and father and his older brother in Baltimore, Maryland.

Thurgood's parents wanted him to be a dentist. They wanted his brother to be a doctor.

In Thurgood's neighborhood, white and black children played together. But they had to go to separate schools. This was called segregation.

Thurgood not only couldn't go to the same school as white children, he had to sit in a special place on the trolley car, and even at the ballpark. Thurgood felt bad about this. But his parents told him that he was as good as anyone else.

Although Thurgood was a bright student,
he was always getting in trouble at school.
His teacher often sent him to the
principal's office.

The principal would make Thurgood
stay after school to read a copy of the
Constitution of the United States. The
Constitution tells how the country should
be governed. In time, Thurgood knew it
almost by heart.

As Thurgood got older, he became interested in law. He and his father would go to the courthouse to watch the trials.

At dinner, Thurgood and his father would
talk about the trials they had seen.

Thurgood and his brother went to Lincoln
University in Pennsylvania. His brother did
very well. In time, he became a surgeon.

At first, Thurgood was more interested in sports and parties than in his studies. Thurgood got in trouble just as he did back in grammar school.

Thurgood had worked hard to get into college. Now he knew it was time to start working hard again.

During his third year in college, Thurgood
met Vivian Burey. Vivian and Thurgood
fell in love and were married.

Thurgood decided to become a lawyer. He applied to the law school at the University of Maryland. But the school turned him down because he was black. So Thurgood went to Howard University in Washington, D.C. instead.

Thurgood graduated from law school in 1933 at the top of his class.

He set up his law office in Baltimore. One day a man named Donald Murray came to see Thurgood.

Like Thurgood, Donald had been turned down by the University of Maryland Law School.

Could Thurgood help him? Thurgood decided to take the University of Maryland to court. Thurgood argued that because the state of Maryland only had one law school, Donald was being denied an equal education.

Thurgood won! The University had to accept Donald Murray.

Thurgood began to fight other states to end
school segregation. He said that African-
American children weren't getting the same
chance for an education as white children.
As an NAACP (National Association for the
Advancement of Colored People) lawyer, he
traveled far and wide to fight segregation.

In 1952, Thurgood fought his biggest battle. The case was called *Brown versus the Board of Education.*

Oliver Brown, a black railroad worker in Topeka, Kansas, was angry because his daughter was not allowed to go to the all-white school near their home. Oliver Brown decided to sue the Topeka school board.

Thurgood's battle took a long time.
Finally, in 1954, the Supreme Court voted
that school segregation was against the
law. No one could force black and white
children to attend separate schools.

Thurgood continued his fight against all
types of segregation—in public parks, on
public transportation, even in the ballparks.

26

In 1964, the Civil Rights Act was passed. It said that every American should receive equal treatment, regardless of race, sex, or color. Segregation had finally ended.

In 1967 President Lyndon B. Johnson asked Thurgood to be one of the nine judges on the Supreme Court. Thurgood was the first black person to become a Supreme Court judge.

The judges of this high court try to
understand the true meaning of the
Constitution. They try to make sure the
words of the Constitution are carried out.

The Supreme Court is the highest court in the country. It began over 200 years ago when the Constitution of the United States was written.

George Washington, Benjamin Franklin, and other important people signed the Constitution. But it is up to the judges on the Supreme Court to make sure our country's laws do what the Constitution says.

Thurgood Marshall always believed in the words of the Constitution. He was proud to serve on the Supreme Court. In his peaceful yet powerful way, he continued to speak out for equal rights for all people until he died in 1993.